BASKETBALL MINDSET
Workbook for girls

Falcon Focus

Table of Contents

WHY MINDSET MATTERS IN BASKETBALL

Basketball is not just a physical game. It is also a mental one. Your skills, speed, and strength matter, but what truly shapes how you play is what is happening in your mind. The way you think before a game, respond to mistakes, and push through tough moments affects both how you play and how much you enjoy the game.

Every dribble, pass, and shot is guided by your thoughts and attitude. A confident mindset helps you stay calm, trust your practice, and make good decisions during the game. Negative thoughts or fear of making mistakes can cause hesitation and frustration, even when you have the ability to do well.

Mistakes are a normal part of basketball. Missed shots, turnovers, and tough games happen to everyone. What matters most is how you respond. A strong mindset helps you reset quickly, stay focused, and keep trying your best.

This book is about building a strong basketball mindset that supports growth, effort, and confidence. When your mind works together with your body, you can play freely, think clearly, and enjoy the game more.

WHAT IS MINDSET?

Mindset is the collection of thoughts, beliefs, and attitudes you have about yourself, your abilities, and your potential. It is the inner voice that talks to you during practice, games, and even after the game is over. In basketball, your mindset shapes how you think, how you act, and how you feel on the court.

In basketball, mindset shapes how you:
- Approach practice and games.
- Handle mistakes and losses.
- Respond to pressure and competition.
- Stay motivated to improve.

Your mindset decides whether challenges feel scary or feel like chances to improve. Missing a shot or losing a game can feel disappointing, but it can also teach you what to work on next. Mindset is not about being perfect or winning every time; it is about effort, attitude, and how you respond when things do not go your way.

The good news is that mindset can be trained, just like dribbling or shooting. With practice, you can learn to think in a positive way, stay confident after mistakes, and keep believing in yourself. A strong mindset helps you grow as a basketball player, a teammate, and a person.

TYPES OF MINDSETS IN BASKETBALL

Understanding different mindsets can help you recognize where you are and what you can improve.

1. FIXED MINDSET

A fixed mindset is when a player believes their ability cannot change. Players with this mindset may avoid challenges, fear mistakes, or give up easily when things get hard. They may think talent is something you either have or do not have.

Common fixed mindset thoughts include:
- "I'm just not good at shooting."
- "If I fail, it means I'm not talented."

This mindset can stop players from trying new skills or improving over time.

2. GROWTH MINDSET

A growth mindset is the belief that skills can improve with effort, practice, and patience. Players with this mindset understand that learning takes time and mistakes are part of getting better.

Examples of growth mindset thinking include:
- "I'm still learning."
- "Mistakes help me improve."

This mindset helps players stay motivated and keep trying, even when things feel challenging.

3. CONFIDENT MINDSET

A confident mindset is about believing in yourself and trusting your preparation. Confident players are not afraid to take smart risks and play their game.

A confident mindset looks like:
- Staying calm under pressure.
- Trusting your training and instincts.

Confidence grows when you practice consistently and believe in your effort.

4. RESILIENT MINDSET

Resilience is the ability to bounce back after mistakes, losses, or tough games. Players with a resilient mindset do not let one bad moment ruin the rest of the game.

This mindset includes:
- Having a short memory after errors.
- Being willing to keep trying.

Resilient players stay strong and focused, no matter what happens.

5. FOCUSED MINDSET

A focused mindset helps players stay in the moment. Instead of thinking about past mistakes or worrying about the final score, focused players pay attention to what they need to do next.

A focused mindset means:
- Paying attention to the next play.
- Staying locked in during practice and games.

Focus helps players make better decisions and play with purpose.

All of these mindset types affect how you play and grow in basketball. Everyone has tough thoughts sometimes, but learning to choose growth, confidence, resilience, and focus helps you improve and enjoy the game more.

STARTING MY BASKETBALL MINDSET JOURNEY

Every basketball journey begins with more than a ball and a hoop. It begins in your mind. How you think about yourself, your effort, and your mistakes plays a big role in how you grow as a player. This chapter is the start of learning how to train your mindset, just like you train your skills.

You do not need to be perfect to begin. You do not need to win every game or make every shot. What matters most is your willingness to learn, try, and keep going even when things feel hard. This book is here to help you build strong thoughts, confidence, and focus, one step at a time.

Basketball is a game of ups and downs. Some days you will feel great on the court, and other days you might struggle. A strong mindset helps you enjoy the game through all of it. This chapter helps you understand where you are starting and where you want to grow.

WHERE I AM RIGHT NOW

Before you can grow as a basketball player, it helps to understand where you are starting. Every player is on a different part of their journey. Some are still learning the basics, while others have had more time to practice and play. None of these are better or worse. They are simply different starting points.

Knowing where you are right now helps you set fair and realistic goals for yourself. It also reminds you not to compare your progress to others. Everyone learns at their own pace. What matters most is your effort, your attitude, and your willingness to keep improving. When you focus on your own path, basketball feels more enjoyable and less stressful.

Take a moment to notice how you feel when you play. Do you feel excited, nervous, confident, or unsure? These feelings are normal, and they can change from day to day. Paying attention to how you feel helps you understand your mindset and gives you a better idea of what you need to work on as you move forward.

ABOUT ME AS A BASKETBALL PLAYER

This section is all about you. Fill in the details below to make this workbook yours and to mark the start of your basketball journey. These answers help you remember where you are right now as a player and how you grow along the way.

This workbook belongs to:

Write it in a style that feels like you. Use neat writing, big letters, bubble letters, cursive, or any style you enjoy.

MY NAME:

MY AGE:

MY SCHOOL OR TEAM:

HOW LONG I HAVE PLAYED BASKETBALL:

A Message to Myself as I Start:

MY BASKETBALL STARTING POINT

Take a moment to think about yourself as a basketball player and answer honestly. There are no right or wrong answers. Write one thing you like about basketball, one thing you want to improve, and one feeling you sometimes have when you play. This is your starting point.

One thing I like about basketball:

____

____

One thing I want to get better at:

____

____

One feeling I sometimes have when I play basketball:

____

____

My Mindset Promise

When basketball feels hard, I will try to:

____

____

____

MY INNER VOICE ON THE COURT

Every basketball player has an inner voice. It is the voice inside your head that talks to you while you play. Sometimes it cheers you on, and sometimes it can be hard or unkind. This chapter helps you notice that voice and learn how to make it more helpful.

Your inner voice can affect how confident you feel, how you handle mistakes, and how much you enjoy basketball. Learning to listen to it and guide it is an important part of building a strong mindset on the court.

When you understand your inner voice, you gain more control over your thoughts and reactions. Instead of letting negative words take over, you can choose words that support your effort and growth. Over time, this practice helps you feel calmer, braver, and more confident each time you step onto the court.

WHAT IS MY INNER VOICE

Your inner voice is the voice inside your head that talks to you when you play basketball. It speaks during practice, games, and quiet moments when no one else is talking. This voice reacts to everything that happens on the court, from making a great shot to missing an easy layup. Sometimes it encourages you and reminds you to keep going. Other times it may sound doubtful or critical. Learning what your inner voice sounds like is the first step to understanding your mindset.

Your inner voice has a strong effect on how you feel and how you play. When it is kind and supportive, you are more likely to feel confident, calm, and willing to try again after a mistake. When it is negative or harsh, it can make you feel nervous, frustrated, or afraid to take chances. This voice often shows up right after mistakes, telling you how to react. Noticing these thoughts helps you understand why some moments feel easy and others feel hard.

The good news is that your inner voice can be trained. Just like basketball skills, it gets better with practice. When you catch unkind thoughts, you can slowly replace them with words that help you stay focused and positive. Over time, your inner voice can become a supportive guide that reminds you to breathe, try again, and believe in yourself. When your inner voice works for you, basketball feels more enjoyable and less stressful.

MY HELPFUL INNER VOICE

The first step to improving your inner voice is learning to notice what it says. Your self talk is the voice inside your head that shows up during practice, games, and quiet moments in between. It reacts to missed shots, tough drills, and big moments. You do not need to judge these thoughts, fix them, or push them away. You simply need to notice them. When you slow down and listen, you begin to understand how your thoughts affect your confidence, focus, and emotions on the court.

Many times, negative thoughts appear quickly and without warning. They can make your body feel tense, your heart beat faster, or your breathing feel shallow. This is when noticing your self talk becomes important. The moment you realize your thoughts are spiraling or becoming unkind, you can pause and reset instead of letting them take over. Awareness gives you choice, and choice gives you control.

As soon as you notice unhelpful thoughts, you can use your calm breathing reset. This is a simple tool you can use anywhere, even during a game. Calm breathing helps your body relax so your mind can slow down too. When your body feels calmer, it is easier to refocus, choose a helpful thought, and move on to the next play.

Use these points to help you notice your self talk:
- What I say after a mistake.
- My thoughts during hard drills.
- My inner voice in close games.
- Whether my self talk is kind or unkind.
- How I talk to myself when I feel tired.
- How my thoughts affect my confidence.

When you notice your thoughts speeding up or turning negative, try this calm breathing reset:

  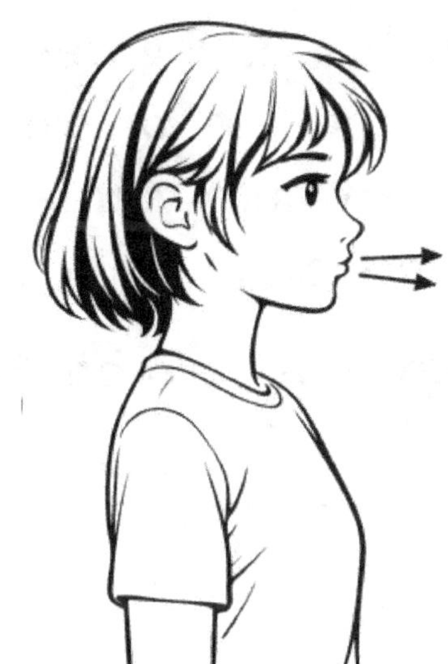

Slowly breathe in through your nose as you count to 4.		Gently breathe out through your mouth as you count to 5.

You can repeat this once or twice. Breathing helps your body settle so your mind can slow down too. When you combine noticing your self talk with calm breathing, you give yourself the power to choose a kinder and more helpful inner voice. This is how your inner voice becomes a supportive teammate, even when things go wrong.

WHERE DO I FEEL MY FEELINGS?

Think about a time you felt nervous, overwhelmed, or stuck in negative thoughts during basketball. Look at the body outline on the page. Color the places where you feel your thoughts or emotions.

The place I colored the most was...

____

____

____

____

When I feel this in my body, it usually means...

____

____

____

One thing I can do to help my body calm down is...

____

____

____

MY INNER VOICE CHECK

Think about a recent practice or game. Notice what your inner voice said and how it made you feel. Answer honestly.

One thing my inner voice says when I do well:

____

____

____

____

How it makes me feel:

| Happy | Calm | Proud | Confident | Unsure |

One thing my inner voice says after a mistake:

____

____

____

____

How it makes me feel:

| Happy | Calm | Proud | Confident | Unsure |

FROM UNKIND TO HELPFUL

Use this page to practice turning unkind thoughts into helpful ones. Write honestly. You can use the same situation or different moments from practice or games.

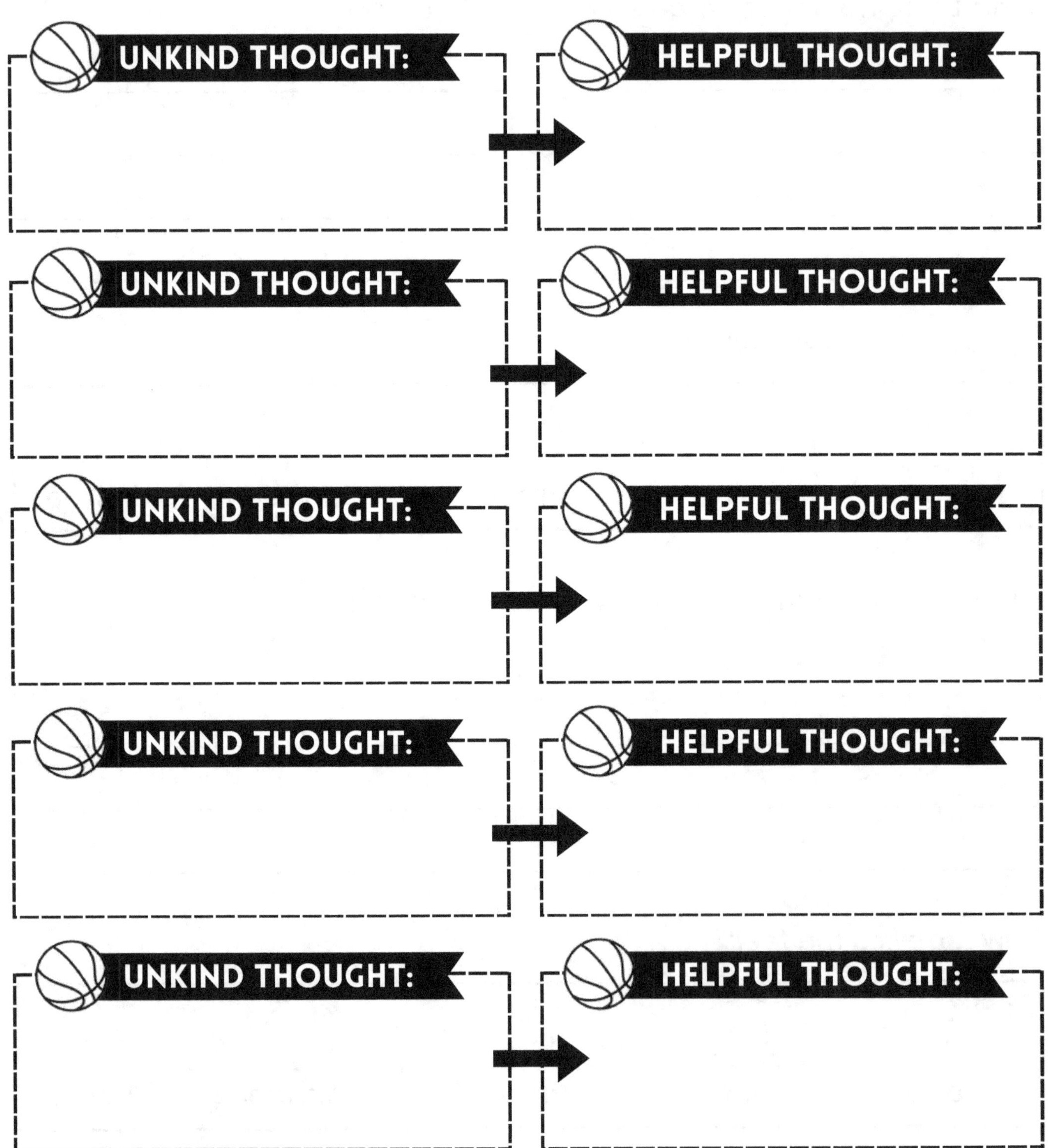

MY ON-COURT REMINDER

Choose one sentence below that you can remind yourself of during games, or write your own reminder. This is something you can think about when you feel nervous, make a mistake, or need encouragement.

- [ ] I can try again.
- [ ] Mistakes help me learn.
- [ ] I am doing my best.
- [ ] I stay calm and focused.
- [ ] I believe in myself.
- [ ] One play at a time.
- [ ] I am learning every day.
- [ ] I keep going even when it is hard.
- [ ] I play with confidence.
- [ ] I trust my practice.

My reminder:

Doodle Page

Sometimes your inner voice is loud. Sometimes it is quiet. This page helps you see what your inner voice sounds like and how you want it to feel. There is no right or wrong way to do this page. You can draw, doodle, write words, or use symbols.

GAME DAY SELF TALK CARD

This is a short message you can carry in your mind on game day. It helps you reset, stay calm, and keep going when the game feels intense.

CONFIDENCE IS BUILT, NOT GIVEN

Confidence in basketball does not appear all at once. It is something you build little by little through effort, practice, and learning from mistakes. Some days you may feel confident, and other days you may feel unsure or nervous. That is completely normal. Every player experiences ups and downs, and every player builds confidence in her own way and at her own pace.

Confidence is not about being the best on the court or playing perfectly every game. It is about trusting yourself enough to keep trying, even when things feel hard. This chapter helps you understand that confidence comes from what you do each day, not from always playing well or getting everything right. Showing up to practice, listening, and giving effort all help confidence grow.

You do not have to wait until you feel confident to try new skills or take chances. Confidence often comes after you try, not before. Each time you push yourself to learn, stay positive after a mistake, or keep going when you feel unsure, you are building confidence. Even when it does not feel big or noticeable, your confidence is growing little by little.

WHERE CONFIDENCE COMES FROM

Confidence grows from small actions that you repeat over time. These actions help you feel prepared, capable, and proud of your effort. Confidence does not come from one great game, one perfect shot, or one compliment from others. It comes from the choices you make every day, especially when things feel hard or uncomfortable.

Confidence grows when you practice regularly, even on days when you feel tired or unmotivated. It grows when you try again after a mistake instead of giving up or getting upset. Staying involved in the game, even when shots are not falling or the score is close, also builds confidence. Each time you choose to keep moving, listening, and trying, you are telling yourself that you can handle challenges.

Confidence is also shaped by how you talk to yourself. Encouraging yourself with kind and helpful thoughts helps you feel calmer and more focused. Supporting your teammates and staying positive builds confidence too, because it reminds you that basketball is about teamwork, effort, and growth, not just individual success.

THE BREAKDOWN OF CONFIDENCE

Confidence is built from different parts working together. When one part feels weak, confidence may feel shaky. When all parts work together, confidence feels stronger.

1. EFFORT

Confidence grows when you try your best, even when things are hard. Giving effort shows you that you can keep going, learn, and improve.

2. PRACTICE

Practice helps you feel prepared. The more you practice skills, the more familiar they feel. This makes you trust yourself during games.

3. MINDSET

Your thoughts matter. A kind and helpful inner voice helps you stay calm, focused, and brave. Negative thoughts can weaken confidence, while positive thoughts help it grow.

4. CONSISTENCY

Doing small things over and over builds trust in yourself. Confidence grows when you keep showing up, not just when you have a good day.

5. RESILIENCE

Confidence gets stronger when you try again after mistakes. Learning to bounce back helps you believe you can handle challenges.

6. SELF-BELIEF

Believing that you can improve helps confidence grow. You do not need to be perfect. You just need to believe that effort leads to growth.

When you understand what builds confidence, you can work on each part. Even strengthening one area can help your confidence grow.

HOW I BUILD CONFIDENCE

Circle or write the things below that feel true for you. Some habits help confidence grow, and some can make confidence feel harder. This activity helps you notice your patterns.

- [ ] Practicing my skills
- [ ] Trying again after mistakes
- [ ] Giving up after a mistake
- [ ] Encouraging myself with kind words
- [ ] Being too hard on myself
- [ ] Staying focused during practice and games
- [ ] Losing focus when things get hard
- [ ] Helping and supporting my teammates
- [ ] Comparing myself to others
- [ ] Listening to my coach
- [ ] Ignoring feedback
- [ ] Giving my best effort
- [ ] Worrying about being perfect
- [ ] Using calm breathing when I feel nervous
- [ ] Believing I can improve
- [ ] Negative self talk
- [ ] Staying involved even when things are not going my way
- [ ] Sitting out mentally after mistakes
- [ ] Celebrating small improvements

CONFIDENCE DOODLE TRAIL

Confidence builds little by little. In the ladder or staircase below, write one thing on each step that helps your confidence grow.

CONFIDENCE

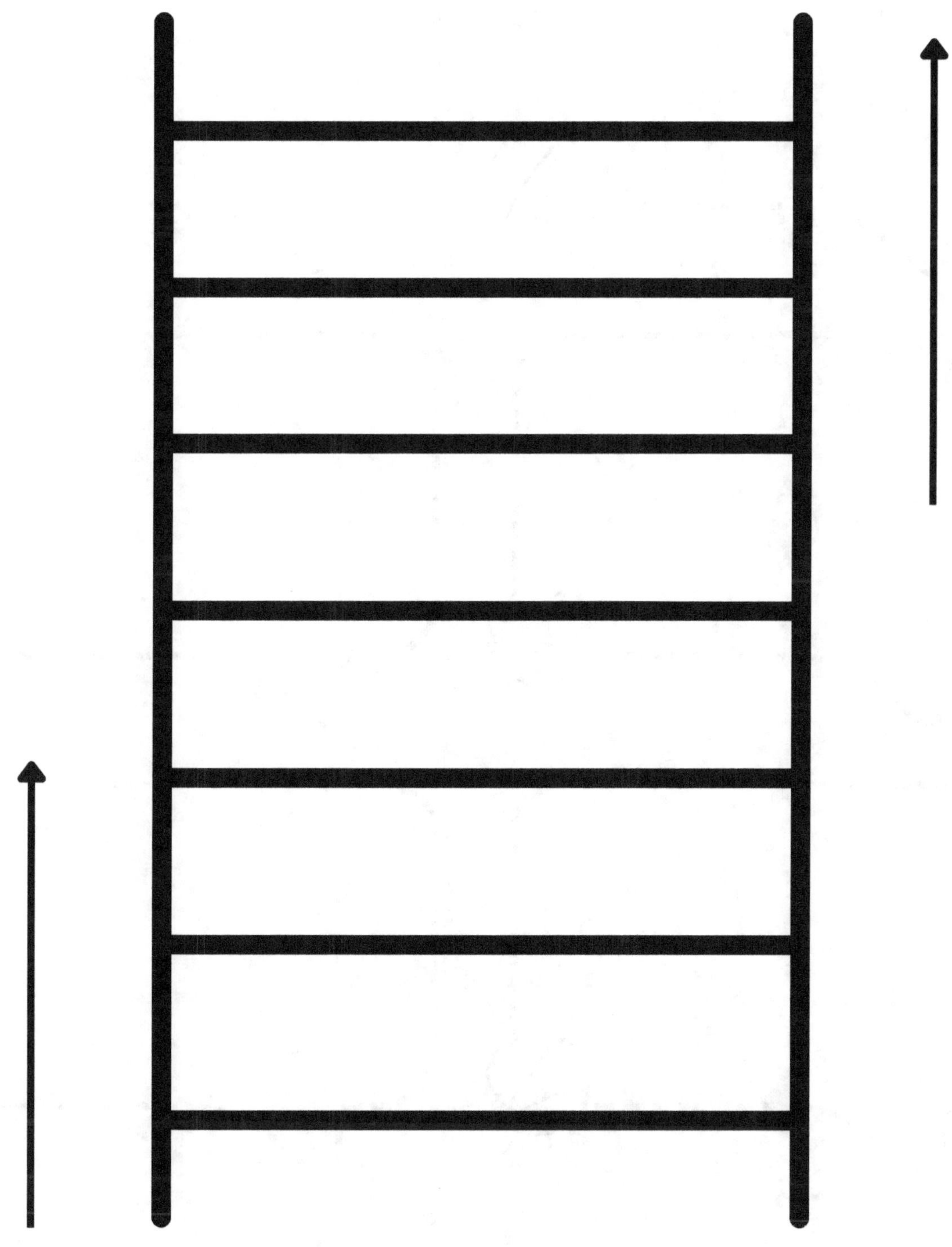

MY CONFIDENCE WORDS

Write the confidence words or phrases you want to remind yourself of during games and practice.

LETTER FROM MY CONFIDENT SELF

Your confident self already exists. Imagine your confident basketball self is writing you a short note.

Dear Me,

____

____

____

____

____

____

____

____

____

____

____

____

My Confident Self

WHEN PLAYS DON'T GO AS PLANNED

Every basketball player has moments when things do not go the way they hoped. A shot may miss, a pass may be off, or a play may fall apart. These moments can feel frustrating, but they are a normal part of the game. They do not mean you are a bad player or that you are failing.

What matters most is how you respond when this happens. When plays do not go as planned, your thoughts and actions can either help you move forward or make the moment harder. Taking a calm breath, staying focused, and reminding yourself to keep going help you reset quickly.

Mistakes and missed plays are chances to learn. Each one teaches you something new about timing, effort, or focus. When you choose to stay involved, support your teammates, and try again, you are building confidence and resilience. One play does not define you. The next play is always a new opportunity.

MISTAKES HAPPEN TO EVERYONE

Mistakes happen to everyone in basketball. Missing a shot, making a bad pass, or turning the ball over does not mean you are bad at the game. It means you are playing, learning, and pushing yourself to improve. Every player, no matter how skilled or experienced, makes mistakes during games and practice. These moments can feel frustrating or disappointing, but they are a normal and important part of growth. Mistakes help you learn what to adjust, what to practice, and how to become a better player.

When a play does not go as planned, your body and mind may react quickly. You might feel your heart beat faster, your shoulders tighten, or your thoughts rush. You may feel upset, nervous, or disappointed with yourself. Learning to stay calm in these moments helps you stay in control. Taking a slow breath, standing tall, or reminding yourself to reset can help your body relax and your mind slow down. Staying calm makes it easier to think clearly and stay confident, even after a mistake.

Basketball moves fast, and there is always another play waiting. You do not have time to stay stuck on one moment. Shifting your focus to the next play helps you stay involved and confident. The next pass, the next step on defense, or the next shot is always a fresh chance to try again. When you learn to let go of mistakes and focus on what comes next, you play with more freedom, confidence, and enjoyment.

MENTAL STRENGTH ON THE COURT

Mental strength is what helps you stay steady when basketball feels challenging. It allows you to keep going when you miss a shot, feel pressure, or face a tough moment in the game. Mental strength does not mean you never feel upset, nervous, or disappointed. Those feelings are normal. What matters is how you respond to them. When you learn to pause, breathe, and refocus, you give yourself the chance to stay in control and keep playing with confidence.

Mental strength looks like:
- Staying calm after a mistake.
- Taking a deep breath to reset.
- Using kind and helpful self-talk.
- Focusing on the next play.
- Keeping effort high even when frustrated.
- Staying involved in the game.
- Trusting yourself to learn and improve.
- Letting go of one bad moment.

Mental strength grows every time you practice these habits. Each calm breath, positive thought, and focused decision helps you become stronger on the court. Over time, mental strength helps you enjoy the game more, handle pressure better, and feel proud of how you show up, no matter what happens during the game.

SIMPLE RESETS FOR BASKETBALL

When something goes wrong on the court, a quick reset can help you calm down and stay focused.

These resets are quick and easy. You can practice them during training so they feel natural in games.

MY QUICK RESET PLAN

Choose what helps you reset when a play does not go as planned.

After a mistake, I can:
- Take one deep breath.
- Say a calm word like "next" or "reset."
- Hustle back on defense.
- Focus on helping my team.

One reset I want to practice:

____

____

Before reset:

After reset:

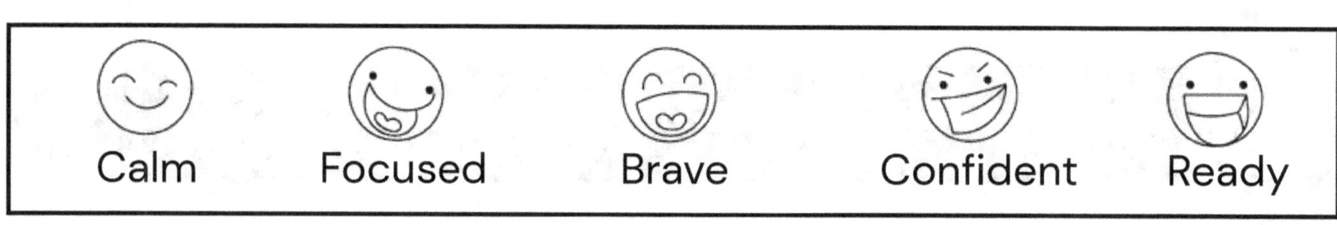

One thing that helps me move from before to after:

____

____

MY BOUNCE BACK MOMENT

Think about a time you recovered after something went wrong.

What happened:

____

____

____

____

What I did next:

____

____

____

____

How I felt after I kept going:

____

____

____

____

PLAYING THROUGH NERVES

Feeling nervous before or during a basketball game is normal. Many players feel butterflies in their stomach, shaky hands, tight shoulders, or fast thoughts. These feelings can show up before tip-off, during a big moment, or after a mistake. Nerves do not mean you are not ready or that something is wrong with you. Most of the time, they mean you care about the game and want to do well.

This chapter helps you understand what nerves really are and why they show up. Nerves are your body's way of getting ready for something important. Instead of fighting them or trying to make them disappear, you can learn to notice them and keep playing anyway. Feeling nervous does not stop you from being a good player.

You do not need to wait until you feel calm to play well. Many strong players learn how to play through their nerves by using breathing, focus, and helpful self talk. This chapter will help you learn how to stay present, trust your practice, and keep going even when nerves show up. When you learn to play with nerves instead of against them, you build confidence and mental strength on the court.

GETTING TO KNOW MY NERVES

Getting to know your nerves means learning how they show up for you. Nerves can feel different each time, and noticing them helps you understand your body and mind during basketball. Instead of guessing or worrying about how you feel, you can learn to recognize the signs early.

You can get to know your nerves by paying attention to your body. Notice if your heart beats faster, your hands feel shaky, your muscles feel tight, or your breathing changes. These are common signals that nerves are present. Your body is getting ready for action, not telling you to stop.

You can also notice your thoughts. Nerves often show up as fast or worried thoughts like thinking too much about mistakes, the score, or what others might think. When you recognize these thoughts, you can remind yourself to stay focused on the next play.

Finally, notice your energy level. Nerves can feel like extra energy, excitement, or restlessness. When you understand this, you can use that energy to move your feet, stay alert, and play with effort. The more you notice these signs, the easier it becomes to understand your nerves and stay in control during the game.

THE THREE-BREATH RESET

The Three-Breath Reset is a simple and powerful way to calm your body and mind during a game. You can use it at the free throw line, after a mistake, during a timeout, or any short pause in play. It is quiet, quick, and easy to do without anyone noticing. This reset helps you feel more in control when nerves show up and your thoughts start to race.

When you feel nervous, your breathing often becomes fast and shallow, and your body may feel tense. The Three-Breath Reset helps slow everything down. By focusing on your breath, you give your mind something calm to pay attention to instead of worries or pressure. This makes it easier to stay present and confident in the moment.

HOW TO DO THE THREE-BREATH RESET

BREATH ONE:

Breathe in slowly through your nose, then breathe out slowly through your mouth. Let your shoulders drop and release any tension.

BREATH TWO:

Breathe in again, then breathe out even longer. In your head, say a calm word like "steady," "breathe," or "next."

BREATH THREE:

Take one more slow, steady breath. Stand tall, feel your feet on the floor, and bring your focus to the next play.

MY NERVES HAVE A NAME

Giving nerves a name helps make them feel smaller and easier to handle. Imagine your nerves are a character, not a problem.

My nerves' name:

What my nerves feel like:

Fast	Tight	Jumpy	Quiet	Excited	Loud

What my nerves are trying to tell me:

____

____

One thing I can say back to my nerves:

____

____

How I feel after naming my nerves:

____

NERVOUS BUT STILL PLAYING

You can feel nervous and still play well. FInish the sentences honestly.

I feel nervous when:

____

____

____

Even when I feel nervous, I can still:

____

____

____

One time I played through nerves was:

____

____

____

How I felt after I kept playing:

____

____

____

MY PRESSURE MOMENT PLAN

Pressure moments do not surprise strong players. They prepare for them. Choose one pressure moment and plan your response.

A pressure moment for me is:

____

____

____

One thing I do with my body:

____

____

____

One thing I say in my head:

____

____

____

How I feel after using my plan:

____

____

____

MY GAME-DAY CALM ZONE

This page is for drawing, doodling, coloring, or writing. There are no rules. Use the space below to show what helps you feel calm and ready before a game.

LOCKING IN DURING THE GAME

During a basketball game, there is a lot happening at once. Players are moving quickly, coaches are giving instructions, teammates are calling for the ball, and the crowd can be loud. All of this can make it easy to feel distracted or overwhelmed. Locking in means learning how to keep your attention on the game, even when many things are happening around you.

This chapter helps you build skills to stay present, aware, and confident while the game is happening. Locking in does not mean being tense or serious all the time. It means knowing what to focus on, noticing what is happening in your body and mind, and trusting yourself to respond in the moment. When you learn to lock in, the game can feel clearer and more manageable.

In this chapter, you will learn three important skills that help you lock in during games: Focus, Awareness and Visualization

WHAT IS FOCUS?

Focus helps you keep your attention on what matters right now, like the ball, your position, or the next play. It teaches you how to let go of distractions, mistakes, and outside noise so you can stay involved in the game.

WHAT IS AWARENESS?

Awareness helps you notice what is happening inside and around you. This includes noticing your thoughts, feelings, and body signals, as well as what is happening on the court. Awareness helps you recognize when you need to reset, breathe, or refocus.

WHAT IS VISUALIZATION?

Visualization helps you prepare your mind before and during the game. By imagining yourself moving confidently, staying calm, and making good decisions, you help your body know what to do when it is time to play. Visualization builds confidence and helps you feel ready.

Together, focus, awareness, and visualization help you stay locked in, calm, and confident from the first whistle to the final buzzer.

FOCUS ON WHAT MATTERS

Focus helps you stay connected to the game without feeling overwhelmed. During a basketball game, there is a lot happening at the same time. If you try to notice everything, your mind can feel busy or rushed. Locking in does not mean paying attention to everything at once. It means choosing a few important things that help you do your job on the court.

When you focus on what matters, your mind feels calmer and clearer. You know where to look, what to listen for, and how to move. This makes it easier to react quickly and make good decisions. Instead of worrying about mistakes or thinking too far ahead, your attention stays on what is happening right.now.

Examples of focus during a game include:
- Watching the ball so you know when to move or react.
- Listening for your name or a call from your coach or teammate.
- Knowing your role on the court and what is expected of you.
- Staying ready on defense by keeping your knees bent and eyes up.
- Moving to open space when you are on offense to help your team.

Simple focus helps you feel confident and in control. When you know what to focus on, you react faster, stay involved in the game, and play with more purpose from start to finish.

AWARENESS OF THE COURT

Awareness means noticing what is happening around you while you play. It is about keeping your eyes up and your mind alert so you can see teammates, defenders, and open space. Awareness helps you understand where you are on the court and what is happening around you in each moment.

When you build awareness, you can make smarter choices during the game. You may spot an open teammate, move into space at the right time, or help on defense before a problem happens. Awareness allows you to react instead of rush and helps you stay one step ahead.

When you build awareness, you can:
- Make better passes.
- Move to open spots.
- Help your teammates on defense.
- Read where the ball is going.
- Stay in the right position.

Awareness grows with practice and attention. The more you focus and look around during games and drills, the easier it becomes to notice what is happening on the court.

VISUALIZATION TO STAY READY

Visualization means using your imagination to prepare your mind and body for basketball. When you visualize, you picture yourself performing a skill or handling a situation before it happens. You might imagine making a clean pass, taking a strong shot, moving your feet on defense, or staying calm under pressure. Even though you are not physically moving, your brain is practicing the action.

You can use visualization before a game, during warm-ups, while waiting on the bench, or during a short pause in play. Close your eyes or soften your focus and picture yourself playing with confidence and control. Imagine what you see, how your body moves, and how it feels when you succeed. This helps your body feel familiar with the action when it happens in real life.

Visualization also helps calm nerves and improve focus. When you picture yourself doing well, your mind feels more confident and prepared. It reminds you that you have practiced and that you are ready. Over time, using visualization helps you stay locked in, react faster, and step onto the court feeling steady and ready to play.

My Focus Spotlight

Focus is like a spotlight that shines on what matters. Draw a big spotlight on the court. Inside the light, draw or write what you want to focus on during the game.

Ideas to include:
- The ball
- Defense
- Teammates
- Effort
- Your feet or hands

Outside the spotlight, you can draw distractions fading away.

Court Awareness Map

Awareness means seeing what is around you. Draw a basketball court. Place yourself on it. Draw teammates, defenders, and open space using simple shapes or symbols.

You can use:
- Arrows to show movement
- Circles for open space
- Lines to show passing options

VISUALIZATION STORYBOARD

This activity helps you picture yourself staying focused and confident during a game. You can draw, doodle, or write a few words in each box.

BEFORE I STEP ON THE COURT

What do I see or feel as the game is about to start?

____

____

____

____

FRAME 1

I LOCK IN

What am I focusing on once the game begins?

____

____

____

____

FRAME 2

A CHALLENGE HAPPENS

Something small goes wrong.
What happens?

____

____

____

____

MY RESET

How do I reset and keep
going?

____

____

____

____

I KEEP PLAYING

What does the next good
moment look like?

____

____

____

____

FRAME 3

FRAME 4

FRAME 5

BUILDING TRUST
WITH MY TEAM

Basketball is a team sport, which means no one plays alone on the court. Every pass, screen, rebound, and word of encouragement matters. When players trust each other, the game feels smoother, calmer, and more connected. Trust helps you feel supported, especially during tough moments.

Trusting your team does not mean everything will always go perfectly. There will be missed shots, mistakes, and disagreements. That is part of playing together. What matters is knowing that your teammates are trying, learning, and growing just like you are. When trust is strong, mistakes feel easier to move past.

This chapter helps you understand how teamwork really works and why every role on the court is important. Not everyone scores the most points, but everyone contributes in meaningful ways. Trust grows when players respect each other's effort and roles.

You will also learn how to handle disagreements and frustrations in a healthy way. Trusting your team helps you enjoy basketball more, feel less pressure, and grow not only as a player, but as a teammate too.

PLAYER POSITIONS AND ROLES

Every player has a role on the team, and each role helps the game flow smoothly. Some players bring the ball up the court, some focus on scoring, and others protect the basket or create space for teammates. No role is more important than another. Basketball works best when everyone understands their role and gives effort to it.

Knowing your position helps you feel more confident and connected on the court. When you understand what your job is, you know where to be, how to help your teammates, and how to stay involved in the game. Roles can change from game to game, and learning different roles helps you grow as a player.

Here are the main basketball positions and what they usually do:

1. POINT GUARD (PG)

The point guard is often called the team leader on the court. She brings the ball up, starts plays, and helps teammates get into the right spots. A point guard looks for open players, makes smart passes, and stays calm under pressure.

2. SHOOTING GUARD (SG)

The shooting guard focuses on scoring and spacing the floor. She looks for good shots, moves without the ball, and helps stretch the defense. Shooting guards also play defense and help bring energy to the team.

3. SMALL FORWARD (SF)

The small forward is a flexible player who can do many things. She may score, rebound, pass, and defend. Small forwards often help wherever the team needs them most and are important all-around players.

4. POWER FORWARD (PF)

The power forward plays strong near the basket. She helps with rebounding, defense, and setting screens. Power forwards use strength and effort to help the team gain possession and create scoring chances.

5. CENTER (C)

The center usually plays closest to the basket. She protects the rim, blocks shots, rebounds, and scores inside. Centers help anchor the defense and give the team strength in the paint.

Every position matters, and teams need all roles working together to succeed. When you take pride in your role and support your teammates in theirs, the whole team becomes stronger.

HOW WE WORK TOGETHER

Team dynamics describe how teammates interact, communicate, and support one another on and off the court. Every team is made up of different personalities, strengths, and energy levels. Some players are loud and encouraging, while others lead by example through effort and focus. Learning how to work together helps everyone feel included and valued.

Strong team dynamics are built on communication and respect. Encouraging words and positive body language help teammates feel supported, especially during tough moments. Simple actions like clapping, giving a thumbs-up, or saying "good job" can lift team energy and confidence. When players feel supported, they are more willing to try, learn, and stay involved.

Listening is another important part of healthy team dynamics. Paying attention to coaches' instructions and teammates' calls helps the team stay organized and connected. Good listening shows respect and helps everyone understand their roles and responsibilities during the game.

Helping each other after mistakes is also key. Missed shots and turnovers happen to everyone. Strong teams respond by encouraging one another instead of blaming. When teammates work together, communicate kindly, and support each other through challenges, the whole team becomes stronger, more confident, and more united.

HANDLING TEAM DISAGREEMENTS

Disagreements can happen on any team. Players may feel frustrated, misunderstand each other, or have different ideas about what should happen during a play. These moments are normal, especially in a fast and emotional game like basketball. Having a disagreement does not mean someone is a bad teammate or that the team is failing.

Healthy teams handle disagreements with respect and self-control. Taking a breath before reacting, listening to the other person, and keeping your voice calm can help prevent small problems from turning into bigger ones. It is important to focus on solving the problem, not blaming each other. Respectful communication helps everyone feel heard and valued.

Disagreements do not mean your team is broken. They are chances to learn more about each other and grow stronger together. When teammates work through disagreements in a positive way, trust improves, teamwork gets stronger, and the team becomes more connected both on and off the court.

MY ROLE ON THE TEAM

Think about your role honestly. Every role gets its moment to shine.

The role I play most often:

____

____

One strength I bring in this role:

____

____

____

____

One role I want to understand better:

____

____

____

____

How I feel when I focus on my role:

____

____

____

____

Communication Bubbles

Good teams talk and listen. In the speech bubbles, write helpful words and encouraging phrases.

OUR TEAM PROMISE

Each player writes her own promise to support the team.

As a teammate, I promise to...

PLAYER NAME

MY PROMISE

PREPARING FOR TIP-OFF

Tip-off is the start of the game, but preparation begins long before the ball goes into the air. How you get ready before the game affects how you feel when it begins. Preparation helps your body feel loose and ready to move, and it helps your mind feel calm and focused instead of rushed or overwhelmed.

Everyone prepares differently. Some players like quiet time, while others like talking or moving around. There is no one "right" way to prepare. What matters is finding simple habits that help you feel steady, confident, and ready to play when the game starts.

This chapter is about creating small, helpful routines that support you before tip-off. You do not need to feel perfect, fearless, or completely calm. Feeling nervous is okay. Being prepared means knowing how to settle your body, focus your mind, and step onto the court ready to give your best effort.

PREPARING FOR TIP-OFF MEANS

Preparing for tip-off means getting both your body and your mind ready to play. Your body needs to warm up so you can move safely and confidently. Your mind needs time to focus, slow down, and settle into the game. When both are prepared, you feel more in control.

Physical preparation includes stretching, light movement, and warming up your muscles. This helps your body feel strong, loose, and ready to react. A good warm-up also helps reduce nerves because your body already feels active and engaged.

Mental preparation is just as important. This includes calming your breathing, focusing your thoughts, and reminding yourself of what matters most. Instead of thinking about winning, mistakes, or pressure, mental preparation helps you focus on effort, teamwork, and the first few plays of the game.

Good preparation helps you start the game with focus instead of rushing or overthinking. When you take time to prepare, you give yourself a smoother transition into the game. You step onto the court feeling ready, grounded, and confident in your ability to play, learn, and keep going from the very first tip-off.

GETTING MY BODY READY

Before the game or practice begins, your body needs movement to feel ready and confident. Warming up helps wake up your muscles, loosen your joints, and get your energy flowing. When your body feels prepared, it becomes easier to move smoothly, react quickly, and play with better balance and control on the court.

A good warm-up also prepares your mind. As you start moving, your body shifts into game mode and your focus improves. Your breathing becomes steadier, your nerves begin to calm, and your attention moves away from distractions and toward the game. Warming up is not about rushing or trying to be perfect. It is about giving yourself time to feel settled and ready before the action begins.

Warming up should feel active but comfortable. You want to move with intention, not push your body too hard or too fast. Light movement increases blood flow, stretching helps your muscles feel loose, and ball touches help you reconnect with the game. Together, these pieces help your body feel confident and prepared.

This warm-up is designed to be simple and easy to follow for players of all levels. You do not need to rush through it. Take your time, move with purpose, and pay attention to how your body feels. When you warm up with care and focus, you step onto the court feeling steady, confident, and ready to play your best.

LIGHT MOVEMENT

Light movement helps wake up your body and get your blood flowing before the game. These exercises gently prepare your muscles and joints so you feel loose, active, and ready to move. Move at a comfortable pace and focus on control, not speed.

JOG AROUND THE COURT

Jog at an easy pace to warm up your legs and increase your heart rate. Keep your breathing steady and relaxed.

HIGH KNEES OR SKIPPING

Lift your knees high or skip lightly across the court. This helps activate your legs and adds energy to your warm-up.

SIDE SHUFFLES

Shuffle side to side while staying low in an athletic stance. This prepares your body for defensive movements.

ARM SWINGS AND SHOULDER CIRCLES

Swing your arms forward and backward, then make slow circles with your shoulders. This helps loosen your upper body and prevent stiffness.

STRETCH AND ACTIVATE

Stretching and activating your muscles helps your body feel loose, strong, and ready to move. These exercises prepare your legs and joints for running, jumping, and changing direction during the game. Move slowly and with control. You should feel a gentle stretch, not pain.

GENTLE LEG SWINGS

Swing one leg forward and back, then side to side. Keep your body tall and controlled.

CALF STRETCHES

Step one foot back and press your heel toward the floor. This helps loosen your lower legs.

QUAD AND HAMSTRING STRETCHES

Gently stretch the front and back of your legs. These muscles work hard during running and jumping.

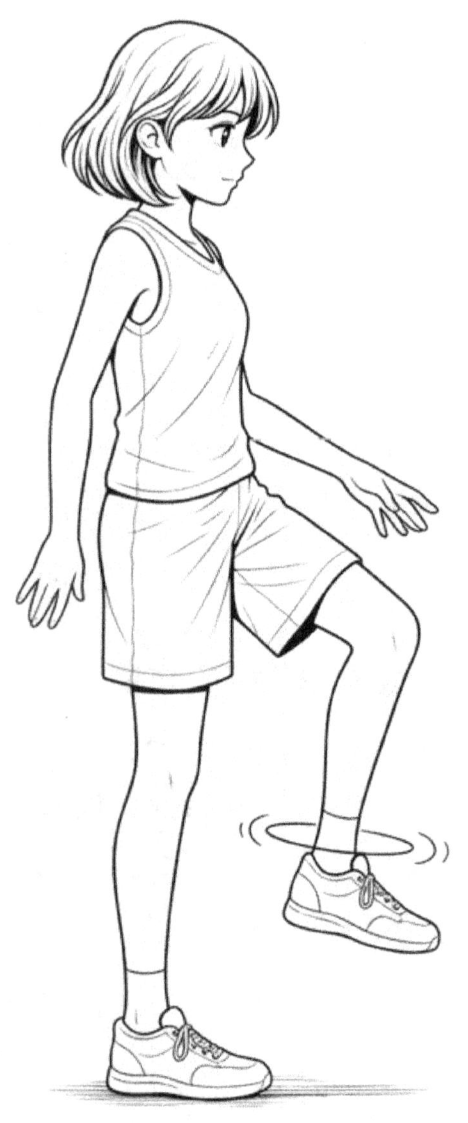

ANKLE CIRCLES

Lift one foot and slowly circle your ankle in both directions. This helps prepare your ankles for quick movements.

BALL TOUCHES

Ball touches help you reconnect with the ball and build confidence before the game begins. These exercises help your hands feel comfortable, your timing improve, and your movements feel smooth. Keep the pace relaxed and focus on control, not speed.

EASY DRIBBLING WITH BOTH HANDS

Dribble slowly and softly using your right and left hand. Keep your eyes up and feel the ball in your fingertips.

PASSING WITH A PARTNER

Make clean, controlled passes back and forth. Focus on accuracy and catching the ball with soft hands.

LAYUP LINES AT A RELAXED PACE

Practice layups without rushing. Focus on good footwork, balance, and finishing with control.

LIGHT SHOOTING CLOSE TO THE BASKET

Take short shots near the hoop to warm up your shooting form. Pay attention to your balance and follow-through.

BASKETBALL FITNESS: MOVING WITH PURPOSE

Basketball fitness is not about pushing your body too hard or trying to be the fastest or strongest player on the court. It is about learning how to move with control, balance, and intention. When your body feels prepared and supported, it becomes easier to focus, play confidently, and enjoy the game without feeling overwhelmed or exhausted.

This chapter helps you understand how simple fitness movements connect directly to basketball. Running, stopping, changing direction, jumping, and staying balanced all require strength, coordination, and body awareness. Basketball fitness teaches your body how to handle these movements safely and smoothly so you feel more confident during games and practices.

The goal of basketball fitness is not perfection. You do not need to do everything perfectly or compare yourself to others. The goal is learning how to move your body in ways that support your skills and protect your energy. Small, consistent movements help your body feel stronger and more stable over time.

Moving with purpose means paying attention to how your body moves, not just how fast or how hard you move. In basketball, quick movements are important, but control is just as important. When you move with purpose, your body feels more stable, confident, and ready to react.

Purposeful movement helps protect your body. Bending your knees when you stop or land helps absorb impact and lowers the chance of injury. Keeping your balance allows you to change direction smoothly instead of rushing or losing control. Landing softly after jumps helps your joints stay safe and strong.

When you move with purpose, you become more aware of your body. You notice how your feet touch the floor, how your posture feels, and when you need to slow down or reset. This awareness helps you stay focused and confident during games and practices.

Purposeful movement builds trust in your body. When you know how to move safely and smoothly, you feel more confident trying new skills and pushing yourself. Moving with purpose helps you play basketball with strength, control, and confidence.

FITNESS THAT HELPS BASKETBALL SKILLS

Basketball fitness is most helpful when it supports the movements you use in real games. Instead of training your body in ways that feel disconnected, basketball fitness focuses on helping you move better on the court. When your fitness matches what basketball asks your body to do, you feel more confident, balanced, and ready to play.

These fitness skills support important parts of the game and help you move with purpose. They grow through simple, consistent movement over time, not by pushing your body too hard all at once.

Examples include:
- Strong legs for defense and jumping.
- Core strength for balance and control.
- Quick feet for changing direction.
- Endurance for staying active throughout the game.

These skills grow through simple, consistent movement. When you train your body to support basketball skills, the game feels smoother, safer, and more enjoyable.

SIMPLE BASKETBALL FITNESS MOVEMENTS

You can do these movements at home or during practice. Move slowly and stop if something does not feel right.

1. ATHLETIC STANCE HOLD

Helps with balance and defense.

- Stand with feet shoulder-width apart.
- Bend knees slightly.
- Keep chest tall and eyes forward.
- Hold for 15–30 seconds.

2. SQUATS

Helps with leg strength.

- Stand tall with feet shoulder-width apart.
- Lower down like sitting in a chair.
- Keep heels on the floor.
- Stand back up slowly.
- Try 8–12 controlled reps.

3. JUMP AND STICK

Helps with safe landing and control.

- Jump straight up.
- Land softly with bent knees.
- Hold balance for 2 seconds.
- Try 5–8 reps.

4. DEFENSIVE SLIDES

Helps with lateral movement.

- Bend knees slightly.
- Step side to side without crossing feet.
- Stay low and controlled.
- Try 20–30 seconds.

5. PLANK HOLD

Helps with core strength.
- Place hands under shoulders.
- Keep body in a straight line.
- Breathe steadily.
- Hold for 15–30 seconds.

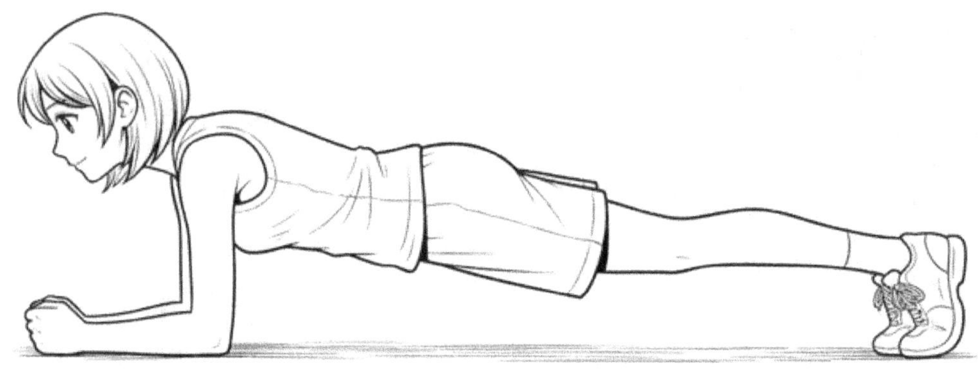

6. SINGLE-LEG BALANCE HOLD

Helps with balance and body control.
- Stand tall on one leg.
- Keep your knee slightly bent.
- Hold your balance and breathe.
- Switch legs.
- Hold for 10–20 seconds on each side.

MY FITNESS CHECK-IN

Answer honestly.

One movement that feels good in my body:

____

____

____

____

One movement I want to practice more:

____

____

____

____

How my body feels after moving:

____

____

____

____

MY PURPOSEFUL MOVEMENT PLAN

Think about the movements that help you feel balanced, strong, or more confident on the court. Choose 2–3 movements to practice this week.

Movement 1: ____

Movement 2:____

Movement 3:____

When I will practice them:

☐ Before practice

☐ During practice

☐ After practice

☐ At home

☐ On specific days:

My goal for these movements:

____

____

____

How I want my body to feel while practicing:

Balanced	Strong	Calm	Confident	Unsure

ASSESSMENT TRACKER

Each session, try to reach the target range listed for each movement. It is okay if you are below or above the target. The goal is effort and steady improvement, not perfection.

Target Guide
- Athletic Stance Hold: 15–30 seconds.
- Squats: 8–12 reps.
- Jump and Stick: 5–8 reps.
- Defensive Slides: 20–30 seconds.
- Plank Hold: 15–30 seconds.
- Single-Leg Balance Hold: 10–20 seconds per leg.
- High Knees March: 20–30 seconds.

Use the target ranges as a helpful guide, not a rule you must follow exactly. Some days your body may feel strong and ready, and other days it may need more rest or shorter effort. Both are okay. Pay attention to how your body feels and focus on good form and control rather than rushing through the movements.

This tracker helps you notice progress over time. If a movement feels easier after a few sessions, that is a sign your body is getting stronger and more confident. If something feels challenging, that is also part of growth. Showing up, trying your best, and moving with purpose are what matter most.

SESSION	ATHLETIC STANCE (SEC)	SQUATS (REPS)	JUMP & STICK (REPS)	DEFENSIVE SLIDES (SEC)	PLANK (SEC)	SINGLE-LEG BALANCE (SEC / LEG)	HIGH KNEES (SEC)
1							
2							
3							
4							
5							
6							
7							
8							
9							
10							

SESSION	ATHLETIC STANCE (SEC)	SQUATS (REPS)	JUMP & STICK (REPS)	DEFENSIVE SLIDES (SEC)	PLANK (SEC)	SINGLE-LEG BALANCE (SEC / LEG)	HIGH KNEES (SEC)
11							
12							
13							
14							
15							
16							
17							
18							
19							
20							

FUELING MY BODY
FOR ENERGY

Basketball takes energy. Your body works hard when you run, jump, defend, and make quick decisions on the court. To do all of this, your body needs fuel. Fuel is what gives you the energy to move, focus, and keep going from the start of the game to the end.

Fueling your body is not about strict rules, dieting, or being perfect. It is about learning what helps your body feel strong, steady, and ready to play. Everyone's body is different, and fueling is about noticing what works best for you. When your body is fueled well, basketball feels more enjoyable and less exhausting.

This chapter helps you understand how food and water support your game before, during, and after basketball. You will learn how fuel helps your body perform, recover, and stay focused. By building simple fueling habits, you give your body what it needs to do its best on and off the court.

FUEL MEANS FOR MY BODY

Fuel is the food and drinks that give your body energy. Just like a basketball needs air to bounce, your body needs fuel to move well. Food provides energy for your muscles, and water helps your body stay balanced and cool while you play.

When you fuel your body well, you may notice that you feel more energized during games and less tired during practice. You may also find it easier to focus, react quickly, and stay positive on the court. Fuel helps your body recover after playing so you are ready for the next practice or game.

Fuel helps your body do what you ask it to do. When your body has enough energy and hydration, it can move with more control, strength, and confidence. Learning how to fuel your body is an important part of taking care of yourself as a basketball player.

GOOD FOODS

These foods help your body feel strong, focused, and ready to move. They are great choices for most days, especially on practice and game days.
- Fruits and vegetables.
- Whole grains like rice, bread, pasta, and oats.
- Protein foods like eggs, chicken, fish, beans, and tofu.
- Dairy foods like milk, yogurt, and cheese.
- Water.

Good foods help you:
- Have energy that lasts.
- Focus better.
- Recover faster after playing.
- Feel strong and steady.

SOMETIMES FOODS

Sometimes foods are okay to eat, but they do not give your body long-lasting energy for basketball. These foods are best enjoyed once in a while, not right before games or practices.

Examples include:
- Candy and sweets.
- Chips and fried foods.
- Sugary drinks.
- Fast food.

Sometimes foods are not bad. They just do not help your body perform its best during basketball.

FOOD GROUPS

Each food group has a job. Eating from different groups helps your body work well.

CARBOHYDRATES (ENERGY FOODS)

Carbohydrates give your body energy to run, jump, and play. Examples:

- Rice, bread, pasta, oats.
- Fruits.
- Some vegetables.

These foods help fuel your muscles and brain.

PROTEIN (MUSCLE HELPERS)

Protein helps your muscles grow and recover after activity. Examples:

- Eggs.
- Chicken, fish.
- Beans, lentils, tofu.

Protein helps your body repair itself after playing basketball.

DAIRY (BONE AND STRENGTH SUPPORT)

Dairy foods help build strong bones and muscles. Examples:

- Milk
- Yogurt
- Cheese

Strong bones help you jump, land, and move safely.

FRUITS AND VEGETABLES (BODY PROTECTORS)

Fruits and vegetables help keep your body healthy and strong.
They provide:

- Vitamins.
- Minerals.
- Fiber.

These foods help your body fight sickness and stay energized.

WATER (HYDRATION)

Water helps your body stay cool and focused.
Water helps:

- Prevent tiredness.
- Keep muscles working.
- Improve focus.

Drinking water before, during, and after playing is very important.

FUELING BEFORE BASKETBALL

Eating before basketball helps give your body the energy it needs to move, focus, and play with confidence. When you eat a small meal or snack before practice or a game, you help your body feel ready instead of tired or sluggish. Fuel before playing gives your muscles and brain the support they need to work together on the court.

Fueling before basketball helps you start strong and keep your energy steady. It can help you run harder, react faster, and stay involved for longer periods of time. When your body has fuel, it is easier to concentrate, listen to your coach, and make good decisions during the game.

Everyone's body is different, so it is important to listen to how your body feels. Some players like to eat a snack closer to practice, while others need more time. Learning what foods and timing work best for you helps you feel confident and prepared each time you play.

Fuel before playing helps you:
- Start strong.
- Stay energized longer.
- Focus better on the court.

FUELING AFTER BASKETBALL

After basketball, your body needs support to recover from all the running, jumping, and effort you put in. Eating and drinking after playing helps your muscles repair and your energy return. This recovery time is just as important as fueling before you play.

Fueling after basketball helps reduce soreness and tiredness. It also helps refill the energy your body used during practice or a game. When you refuel, your body is better prepared for the next day, whether that is another practice, a game, or school activities.

Recovery fuel is part of being a strong athlete. Taking care of your body after playing helps you feel better, move easier, and stay healthy over time. Even a small snack and water can make a big difference.

Fueling after playing helps:
- Reduce soreness.
- Refill energy.
- Prepare your body for the next day.

MY AFTER-BASKETBALL FUEL CHECK

Think about what you usually eat or drink after basketball and how it helps your body recover.

One thing I usually eat or drink after basketball:

____

____

____

How soon I usually refuel after playing:

☐ Right away.

☐ Within 30 minutes.

☐ Later.

How my body feels after I refuel:

☐ Less tired.

☐ Still tired.

☐ Better the next day.

One recovery food or drink I want to try:

____

____

____

AFTER THE FINAL BUZZER

When the final buzzer sounds, the game may be over, but your growth as a player continues. What you do after the game matters just as much as what you do during it. This chapter focuses on how to respond once the court goes quiet and emotions settle. It is about learning from the experience, not judging yourself.

After a game, it is normal to feel many emotions. You might feel proud, disappointed, excited, or frustrated. Wins and losses both bring lessons. Learning how to slow down, reflect, and check in with yourself helps you handle these feelings in a healthy way. This helps you move forward instead of staying stuck in one moment.

This chapter will guide you on how to reflect on your effort and choices, and how to talk to yourself after the game ends. Reflection is not about replaying everything that went wrong. It is about noticing what you learned and what you want to improve next time.

GAME REFLECTION

Reflecting on a game means taking a calm look at your experience after it ends. It is about noticing what went well and what you can learn, not about judging yourself or replaying every moment. You do not need to think about everything that happened. Choosing one positive moment and one learning moment is enough.

Game reflection helps you understand your effort, choices, and growth. When you notice a good moment, you remind yourself of what you did well. When you notice a learning moment, you give yourself a chance to improve without feeling discouraged. Both are important parts of becoming a stronger player.

Reflection helps you grow without being hard on yourself. It turns experience into progress and helps you focus on effort, learning, and improvement. Over time, reflecting after games builds confidence and helps you move forward with clarity and balance.

One thing I did well in this game:

____

____

____

One thing I learned from this game:

____

____

____

AFTER-GAME REFLECTION

For each category below, rate your experience on a scale from 1 to 5, where 1 is the lowest and 5 is the highest.

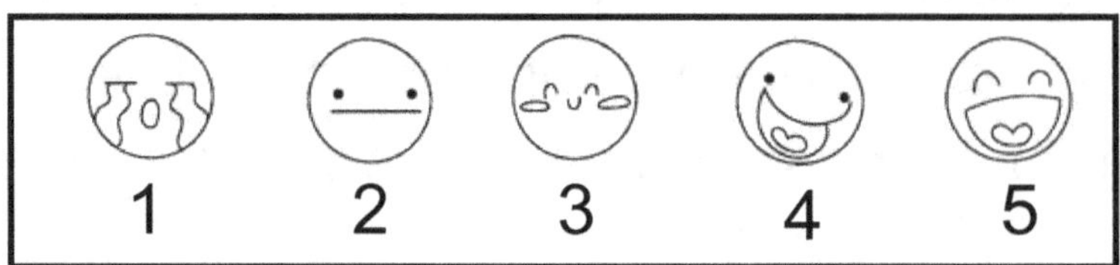

 ## CONFIDENCE

How well did you trust yourself and move on after mistakes?

ENERGY

How steady was your energy from warm-up until the end of the game?

 ## HARDWORK

How much effort and hustle did you give during the game?

 ## COMMUNICATION

How well did you communicate and encourage your teammates?

 ## FOCUS

How well did you stay focused and present while playing?

ATTITUDE

How well did you stay positive and respond to challenges during the game?

After each game, reflect on how you performed in these areas: Energy, Focus, Confidence, Communication, Hard Work, and Attitude . Rate each one on a scale from 1 to 5. Add your ratings to find your Total Score and use it to track your progress from one game to the next.

AFTER-GAME REFLECTION

	Game 1	Game 2	Game 3	Game 4	Game 5
👍					
📣					
🔋					
👁					
👟					
🙂					
Total Score					

	Game 6	Game 7	Game 8	Game 9	Game 10
👍					
📣					
🔋					
👁					
👟					
🙂					
Total Score					

	Game 11	Game 12	Game 13	Game 14	Game 15
👍			89		
📢					
🔋					
👁					
👟					
🙂					
Total Score					

	Game 16	Game 17	Game 18	Game 19	Game 20
👍					
📢					
🔋					
👁					
👟					
🙂					
Total Score					

TWELVE

REST, RECOVERY, AND RESETTING

Playing basketball takes energy, focus, and effort. Your body and mind work hard during practices and games as you run, jump, defend, and make quick decisions. All of that effort adds up. Rest and recovery are what help your hard work turn into strength, confidence, and real progress on the court.

This chapter is about learning how to slow down and listen to your body. Rest is not about being lazy or stopping improvement. It is an important part of training that helps you feel balanced, refreshed, and ready to play again. When you rest well, you give your body and mind the chance to reset and grow.

Rest is not something you earn only after doing enough. It is something your body and mind need regularly to stay healthy and enjoy basketball. Learning when to rest helps you avoid burnout, stay motivated, and keep loving the game.

WHY REST MATTERS

Rest plays a big role in helping your body and mind stay healthy and strong. After practices and games, your muscles need time to recover from running, jumping, and quick movements. Rest gives your body the chance to repair itself, rebuild strength, and prepare for the next time you play. Without enough rest, your body does not have time to fully recover.

Rest also helps your mind. Basketball takes a lot of focus, decision-making, and emotional energy. When you rest, your mind can slow down, reset, and become clearer. This makes it easier to concentrate, stay positive, and manage emotions during games and practices.

Without enough rest, you may notice that you feel more tired, sore, or frustrated. It can become harder to focus, and mistakes may feel more upsetting than usual. You might also lose motivation or enjoyment for the game. These are signs that your body and mind need time to recharge.

Strong players understand that rest is part of training, not a break from it. Rest helps you show up feeling balanced, confident, and ready to give your best effort. When you treat rest as an important part of your routine, you support your growth and make basketball more enjoyable over time.

DIFFERENT TYPES OF REST

Rest comes in different forms, and each type supports your body and mind in a special way. Learning when and how to use each kind of rest helps you recover fully and stay excited about basketball.

1. PHYSICAL REST

Physical rest is what your body needs after hard practices and games. This includes getting enough sleep, taking quiet breaks, or having a full day off from basketball. Physical rest allows your muscles to repair, your joints to recover, and your energy to return. When you give your body proper physical rest, you reduce soreness and lower the risk of injury. Strong players understand that sleep and downtime are just as important as training.

2. ACTIVE REST

Active rest is gentle movement that helps your body recover without pushing too hard. This can include stretching, walking, light yoga, or easy mobility exercises. Active rest keeps your muscles loose and helps blood flow through your body, which supports recovery. It is helpful on days when you feel stiff but not exhausted and still want to move in a calm, relaxed way.

3. MENTAL REST

Mental rest gives your brain a break from basketball thoughts. Thinking about plays, mistakes, or performance all the time can be tiring. Mental rest means stepping away from basketball and doing something different, like reading, drawing, listening to music, or enjoying a favorite hobby. Giving your mind time to reset helps you return to the game feeling focused, clear, and less stressed.

4. EMOTIONAL REST

Emotional rest helps you feel calm, supported, and balanced. This includes having fun, laughing, relaxing, and spending time with people who make you feel good. Emotional rest helps release pressure and reminds you that your worth is not based on performance. When you feel emotionally supported, you play with more joy, confidence, and ease.

All four types of rest work together to support your overall well-being. Sometimes you may need more physical rest, while other times your mind or emotions may need more care. Learning to listen to your body and feelings helps you choose the right kind of rest at the right time.

Rest is not something to feel guilty about. It is a powerful part of becoming a stronger, healthier, and more confident basketball player. When you give yourself permission to rest, you protect your love for the game and set yourself up for long-term growth and enjoyment on and off the court.

RESETTING MY MIND

Your mind needs recovery just like your body does. Thinking about basketball all the time, replaying mistakes, or worrying about future games can feel overwhelming. When your mind is tired, it can be harder to focus, stay positive, and enjoy playing. Resetting your mind helps you step away for a moment so you can come back feeling calmer and more balanced.

A mental reset gives your thoughts space to slow down. This helps reduce stress and clears your head after practices or games. When your mind feels rested, it is easier to concentrate, make decisions, and handle challenges on the court. Mental recovery helps you feel more confident and in control.

A reset does not have to be complicated or take a long time. Simple actions like taking deep breaths, relaxing your body, listening to music, drawing, reading, or spending time with friends can help your mind relax. Doing something you enjoy away from basketball reminds you that rest is part of growing and helps you return to the game feeling fresh, calm, and ready to play again.

MY REST MENU

Fill in each section with ideas that help you rest and recover.

Quick rest (5–10 minutes):

____

____

____

Calm rest (quiet and slow):

____

____

____

Happy rest (makes me smile):

____

____

____

Body rest (helps my muscles):

____

____

____

MY PERFECT RECOVERY DAY

Imagine a day focused on helping your body and mind feel good.

Morning:
What helps me start calm:

____

____

____

Afternoon:
What helps me recharge:

____

____

____

Evening:
What helps me wind down:

____

____

____

How I feel at the end of this day:

____

____

____

TAKING CARE OF MY BODY AND FEELINGS

Playing basketball uses more than just your muscles. It uses your thoughts, emotions, and energy too. You move your body, think quickly, try your best, and care about how you play. Because basketball asks so much from you, it is important to take care of both your body and your feelings.

This chapter is about learning to notice what your body and emotions are telling you. Some days you may feel strong and excited, and other days you may feel tired, sore, or frustrated. All of these feelings are normal. Learning to respond with kindness instead of pushing through everything helps you stay healthy and confident.

Taking care of yourself does not make you weak. It helps you feel safer in your body, more balanced in your emotions, and more confident on and off the court. When you listen to yourself, you give yourself the support you need to keep growing and enjoying basketball.

MY BODY IS COMMUNICATING

Your body is always sending you messages. Feeling tired, sore, hungry, energized, stiff, or uncomfortable are all ways your body communicates with you. These signals are not problems or something to ignore. They are helpful messages that tell you what your body needs.

When you learn to notice your body's signals, you can respond in better ways. Feeling tired may mean you need rest. Feeling sore may mean your muscles need recovery or stretching. Feeling hungry may mean your body needs fuel. Paying attention helps you take action before small issues turn into bigger ones.

Strong players listen to their bodies. They understand that pushing through pain or ignoring signals can lead to injury, burnout, or frustration. When you respect your body's communication, you build trust with yourself and learn how to care for your body in a healthy way.

Listening to your body helps you know when to rest, move, eat, hydrate, or ask for help. This awareness supports your performance, your well-being, and your confidence as a basketball player and as a person.

CONNECTING BODY FEELINGS AND EMOTIONS

Your feelings often show up in your body, even before you fully understand them in your mind. Nervous feelings might feel like a fast heartbeat, shaky hands, or tight shoulders. Frustration can feel like clenched fists, a tight jaw, or tense muscles. Calm and confidence may feel like slow breathing, relaxed shoulders, and steady movement.

Learning to notice these body feelings helps you understand your emotions better. Instead of feeling confused or overwhelmed, you can recognize what is happening and respond with care. Your body gives you clues that help you slow down, breathe, or take a break when needed.

When you understand the connection between your body and emotions, it becomes easier to take care of yourself in the moment. You can choose actions that help you feel safer and calmer, such as taking deep breaths, stretching, or using kind self-talk. This awareness helps you stay balanced and confident both on and off the court.

ASKING FOR SUPPORT

You do not have to handle everything on your own. Basketball can bring excitement, pressure, and strong emotions. Sometimes your body may feel sore or injured, or your feelings may feel heavy, confusing, or overwhelming. When this happens, speaking up is one of the most important things you can do for yourself.

Asking for help is a sign of strength and self-respect. It shows that you are listening to your body and emotions and taking care of yourself. Talking to a trusted adult helps you get guidance, support, and solutions that you might not be able to find on your own. Coaches, parents, teachers, and caregivers want to help you feel safe, healthy, and supported.

Speaking up also helps prevent small problems from becoming bigger ones. A small ache can turn into an injury if ignored. Feelings that stay bottled up can become harder to handle over time. Sharing what you are experiencing allows others to help you find the right support, whether that means rest, adjustments, encouragement, or extra care.

Learning to ask for support builds confidence and trust in yourself. It reminds you that you matter and that your well-being is important. When you speak up, you are taking an active role in caring for your body and feelings, both on and off the court.

MY BODY SIGNALS CHECK-IN

Take a quiet moment to check in with your body. There are no right or wrong answers. Notice how you feel today and answer honestly.

When my body needs rest, it feels:

____

____

____

____

When my body feels ready to move, it feels:

____

____

____

____

One body signal I want to listen to more:

____

____

____

____

NAMING MY FEELINGS

Basketball can bring up many different feelings, and all of them are okay. Take a moment to think about how you usually feel during practices or games. Circle the feelings that match your experience, or write your own if they are not listed.

Circle what you feel during basketball:

Happy   Proud   Nervous   Excited   Tired

One feeling I notice often when I play:

____

____

____

____

One feeling I want to handle more kindly:

____

____

____

____

MY BODY AND FEELINGS MAP

Use the space below to explore how your feelings show up in your body. There is no right or wrong way to do this activity. Take your time and be honest with yourself.

Helpful prompt:
Where do I feel nervous, calm, excited, or tired in my body?

LEARNING FROM MISTAKES

Mistakes are a natural part of learning basketball. Every player makes them, no matter how skilled or experienced they are. Missing a shot, losing the ball, or forgetting a play does not mean you failed. It means you showed up, took a chance, and were part of the game. Without mistakes, learning would not happen.

This chapter helps you understand how to respond to mistakes in a healthy and helpful way. Instead of getting stuck in frustration or self-criticism, you will learn how to use mistakes as tools for growth. How you respond after a mistake matters more than the mistake itself.

Learning from mistakes builds confidence, courage, and resilience both on and off the court. When you know mistakes are part of the process, you feel safer trying new things and pushing yourself to improve. This mindset helps you enjoy basketball more and trust yourself as a growing player.

MISTAKES MEAN I AM LEARNING

Mistakes are an important part of learning basketball. Every time you try something new or push yourself, mistakes can happen. This does not mean you are bad at basketball. It means you are practicing, experimenting, and growing. Learning happens when you are willing to try, even when you might mess up.

Mistakes give you helpful information. They show you what skills need more practice and what adjustments you can make next time. Instead of seeing mistakes as something to feel embarrassed about, you can see them as feedback that helps you improve. Each mistake teaches you something small that adds up over time.

For example, if you miss a shot, you might learn that you need to adjust your balance or follow-through. If you lose the ball while dribbling, you might learn to keep your head up or protect the ball better. If you forget a play, you learn that you need to review it or ask questions during practice. These moments are not failures. They are lessons.

When you understand that mistakes mean learning, you feel less afraid to try. You become more confident, patient, and resilient. Learning players are growing players, and growing players give themselves permission to make mistakes and keep going.

HOW I TALK TO MYSELF

What you say to yourself after a mistake matters a lot. The words in your head can either make the moment harder or help you move forward. Harsh or unkind self-talk can make you feel upset, nervous, or stuck on the mistake. Kind and supportive words help you stay calm, confident, and focused on the next play.

After a mistake, it is easy to be hard on yourself. Thoughts like "I ruined everything" or "I should have done better" can take your attention away from the game. Learning to notice these thoughts gives you the chance to replace them with words that help instead of hurt.

Here are examples of changing harsh self-talk into helpful self-talk:

HARSH SELF-TALK	HELPFUL SELF-TALK:
"I messed up"	"Everyone makes mistakes. I can try again."
"I am bad at this"	"I am still learning."
"I always mess up"	"One mistake does not define me."
"I should not have shot that"	"I was being brave and taking a chance."
"I can't do this"	"I can reset and keep going."

MISTAKES ARE PART OF MY STORY

Take a moment to think about a mistake you have made in basketball. Remember that mistakes are part of learning and growing. Answer honestly and take your time.

One mistake that helped me improve:

____

____

____

____

____

____

One thing mistakes have taught me about myself:

____

____

____

____

____

____

HARD WORDS TO HELPFUL WORDS

Think about something you sometimes say to yourself after a mistake or tough moment in basketball. Write it down, then practice changing it into words that help you move forward and stay confident.

HARD WORDS	HELPFUL WORDS

SEEING MY PROGRESS OVER TIME

Progress in basketball does not always happen quickly or in a straight line. Some days you may feel strong, confident, and proud of how you play. Other days may feel frustrating or difficult. Both types of days are part of learning and growing as a player. Progress includes all of it.

This chapter helps you learn how to notice your growth over time instead of focusing only on one game or one moment. Progress is not only about points scored, wins, or statistics. It also shows up in effort, mindset, confidence, and how you respond when things feel challenging.

Learning to see your progress helps you stay motivated and kind to yourself. When you notice how far you have come, even in small ways, you build confidence and trust in your journey. Progress happens when you keep showing up, learning, and believing in yourself.

WHAT PROGRESS REALLY LOOKS LIKE

Progress in basketball is more than making shots or winning games. It shows up in many small moments that may not always be obvious. Progress can look like trying again after a missed shot, staying focused after a turnover, listening more closely during practice, or feeling a little calmer when the game gets intense. These moments may seem small, but they are important signs that you are growing.

Progress is also not a straight line. Some days you may feel confident and play well, and other days may feel frustrating or harder than usual. For example, you might have a great game one week and then struggle the next. This does not mean you are getting worse. It means you are learning, adjusting, and continuing your journey. Growth often includes ups and downs, and both are part of improvement.

Sometimes progress is quiet and easy to miss. You may not notice that you are improving because change happens little by little. You might not see it right away, but you may react faster than before, recover from mistakes quicker, or believe in yourself more than you used to. These small wins add up over time.

When you understand what progress really looks like, you stop comparing yourself to others and focus on your own path. Everyone grows at a different pace. Every step counts, even the hard days. Each effort, lesson, and moment of growth builds confidence and helps you become a stronger, more resilient basketball player.

NOTICING CHANGES BEYOND SKILLS

Progress does not only show up in your physical skills. It also shows up in how you feel, think, and respond during basketball. These changes are just as important as learning new moves or improving your shooting.

You might notice progress when:
- You stay calmer after mistakes.
- You recover faster when something goes wrong.
- You feel more confident speaking up.
- You communicate better with teammates.
- You understand the game more clearly.
- You feel less nervous in tough moments.
- You believe in yourself more than before.

These changes may feel quiet, but they matter a lot. Mental and emotional growth helps you stay confident, focused, and resilient on the court. When you notice progress beyond skills, you learn to appreciate your full growth as a basketball player and as a person.

EVERYONE'S JOURNEY IS DIFFERENT

Every basketball player grows at a different pace, and that is completely normal. Some players improve quickly in certain areas, while others take more time. Everyone starts from a different place and learns in their own way. There is no single timeline for growth.

Comparing yourself to others can make it hard to see your own progress. You may overlook the effort you are putting in or the small improvements you are making because you are focused on someone else's journey.

MY PROGRESS TIMELINE

Progress happens over time. Draw a line across the page to show your basketball journey so far. Add moments along the line.
You can include:

- When you started playing.
- A tough moment.
- A moment you felt proud.
- A recent improvement.

Label each moment with a word, symbol, or short sentence.

THE GROWTH JAR

Imagine your progress is stored in a jar. Each time you grow, you write something to add to the jar.

If my jar was full of progress, it would include:
- One effort I made:
- One mistake I learned from:
- One time I kept going:
- One moment I felt confident:

LOOKING AHEAD WITH CONFIDENCE

Setting goals is about choosing something that supports your learning and effort. When your goals are kind and realistic, they help you stay focused and proud of your progress. Remember, growth is not about rushing. It is about showing up and trying again.

Set one gentle goal for your future growth.

One thing I want to keep working on:

____

____

One habit that helps my progress:

____

____

One skill I want to feel more confident in:

____

____

One mindset I want to practice more often:

____

____

One way I will encourage myself when things feel hard:

____

BASKETBALL CHALLENGES AND SKILL BUILDERS

Basketball skills grow through practice, patience, and play. Challenges are a fun and motivating way to build skills while staying curious and confident. Instead of worrying about doing everything perfectly, challenges help you focus on effort, learning, and trying your best.

This chapter is about using small, positive challenges to improve your basketball skills. These challenges give you something clear to work toward and help you stay engaged during practice. They also help you notice progress over time, even when improvement feels slow.

Basketball challenges are not about being the best player or comparing yourself to others. They are about getting better at your own pace. Each challenge is a step forward, helping you build confidence, consistency, and enjoyment in the game.

SKILL CHALLENGE

Skill challenges help you practice with purpose. Instead of doing drills without a goal, challenges give you something specific to focus on. This makes practice feel more fun and meaningful, and it helps you stay motivated.

Challenges help you stay focused during practice because you know what you are working toward. They also build confidence through effort. Each time you try, even if you do not succeed right away, you are learning and improving. The effort you put in matters more than the result.

Skill challenges also teach you how to learn from trying. You may not complete a challenge the first time, and that is okay. Challenges remind you that progress comes from practice, patience, and repetition.

Every challenge is a chance to grow. When you take on challenges with a positive mindset, you build skills, confidence, and resilience that help you both on and off the court.

You do not need to complete every challenge perfectly for it to matter. Basketball skill building is about effort, not perfection. Each time you try, you are giving your body and mind a chance to learn, even if the result is not exactly what you hoped for.

Some days challenges will feel easier, and other days they will feel harder. This is normal. Hard days do not mean you are getting worse. They often mean you are stretching your skills or learning something new. Both easy and hard days help you improve.

SKILL BUILDER CHALLENGES

These challenges turn practice into a game. You can try them at home, at practice, or during free time. Pick one or two challenges to work on at a time and give them your best effort. There is no rush and no pressure. The goal is to try, learn, and have fun while building confidence.

Think of each challenge as a mini mission. Every time you try one, you are training your body, your focus, and your confidence.

DRIBBLING BUILDER

Mission: Become more comfortable with the ball.
- Dribble with your right hand for 30 seconds.
- Switch to your left hand for 30 seconds.
- Try to keep your eyes up and stay relaxed.

Bonus challenge: Can you stay low and quiet with the ball?

PASSING BUILDER

Mission: Improve accuracy and control.
- Pass the ball to a wall or target 10 times.
- Aim for the same spot each time.
- Catch the ball softly and reset before the next pass.

Bonus challenge: Count how many clean passes you make in a row.

SHOOTING BUILDER

Mission: Build confidence in your shot.
- Take 5 shots from a comfortable spot.
- Set your feet, bend your knees, and follow through.
- Take a deep breath before each shot.

Bonus challenge: Notice how many shots feel smooth, not how many go in.

FOOTWORK BUILDER

Mission: Stay light, quick, and balanced.
- Do quick steps in place for 20 seconds.
- Stay on the balls of your feet with knees bent.
- Keep your body under control.

Bonus challenge: Can you stay balanced the whole time?

Every challenge you try helps you grow. Some days will feel easy, and some days will feel hard. Both count. Skill building is about effort, curiosity, and showing up — not being perfect.

CHALLENGE TRACKER

Use this tracker to record your challenge attempts. Focus on effort, control, and confidence. After each attempt, write a number for each skill, where 1 means Needs work, 2 means Getting better, and 3 means Felt strong.

CHALLENGE ATTEMPT	DRIBBLING BUILDER	PASSING BUILDER	SHOOTING BUILDER	FOOTWORK BUILDER	TOTAL SCORE
1					
2					
3					
4					
5					
6					
7					
8					
9					
10					
11					
12					
13					
14					
15					

SETTING GOALS FOR MY GAME

Goals help give your basketball journey direction. They remind you what you are working toward and help you stay motivated, even when things feel hard or progress feels slow. Goals are not about being perfect, winning every game, or never making mistakes. They are about learning, growing, and giving your best effort over time.

This chapter helps you learn how to set goals that feel supportive, realistic, and achievable. Good goals help you focus on what you can control, such as effort, attitude, and consistency. When goals are clear and kind, they build confidence instead of pressure and help you enjoy basketball more.

Setting goals also helps you notice progress that you might otherwise miss. When you know what you are working toward, it becomes easier to see improvement and stay encouraged, even on challenging days.

WHAT GOALS ARE REALLY FOR

Goals help you focus your energy and attention on what matters most. Instead of feeling unsure about what to work on, goals give you a clear direction. They help you show up to practice with purpose and make your effort feel meaningful, even on days when basketball feels challenging.

A good goal does not add stress or pressure. It does not rush you or make you feel judged. Instead, it gently guides your effort and reminds you what you are learning. Goals help you focus on things you can control, like effort, attitude, and consistency, rather than worrying about results you cannot control.

Good goals:
- Help you stay motivated, especially on hard days.
- Give purpose to practice and repetition.
- Help you notice progress, even in small steps.

Goals are tools to guide you, not rules to judge you. They are meant to support your growth, not make you feel bad if things do not go perfectly. When you use goals the right way, they help you build confidence, enjoy basketball more, and trust your journey as a growing player.

BIG GOALS AND SMALL GOALS

Big goals can feel exciting and inspiring. They often focus on something you want to improve over time, like becoming a better shooter, feeling more confident during games, or staying calmer under pressure. Big goals give you a long-term direction and remind you what you are working toward.

Small goals help you reach those big goals step by step. They focus on actions you can take right now and repeat often. Small goals are easier to work on, easier to track, and help you feel successful along the way. Each small goal builds confidence and keeps you moving forward.

Small goals might include:
- Practicing a skill a few times each week.
- Staying positive and kind to yourself after mistakes.
- Listening closely and following instructions during practice.

Big goals are long-term goals. They focus on who you want to become as a player over time.

Examples of big goals:
- Become more confident during games.
- Improve my ball handling.
- Feel calmer under pressure.
- Be a supportive and positive teammate.
- Enjoy basketball more and try my best.

Big goals give you direction, but they take time.

MY BASKETBALL GOALS

Use this space to doodle or draw your goals instead of writing them. Sketch pictures, symbols, or simple drawings that show what you want to work toward in basketball.

One goal I have for this season:

One goal I have for practice:

One goal I have for games:

BIG GOAL, SMALL STEPS

Choose one big basketball goal and break it into smaller steps you can practice over time. Small steps make big goals feel easier and more achievable.

My big goal:

____

____

____

Small Step 1:

____

____

Small Step 2:

____

____

Small Step 3:

____

____

THE PLAYER I'M BECOMING

Basketball is more than a game you play. It is a journey that helps shape who you are becoming, both on and off the court. Every practice, every challenge, every mistake, and every win teaches you something about yourself. Each experience adds to your growth.

This final chapter is about looking back at how far you have come and looking forward with confidence. It is a chance to notice your effort, your learning, and the ways you have grown, even when progress felt slow or difficult.

This chapter is also a reminder that growth never stops. You are always learning, improving, and becoming stronger. What matters most is that you keep showing up with effort, courage, and belief in yourself.

WHAT I'VE LEARNED ABOUT MYSELF

Through basketball, you have learned many things about yourself that go beyond skills and drills. You have learned how your body feels when it is tired, strong, or ready to move. You have learned how your mindset can help you stay focused, confident, and calm, even during challenging moments.

Basketball also teaches you about your emotions. You learn how to handle nervous feelings, how to respond after mistakes, and how to keep going when things feel hard. Each time you try again, support a teammate, or speak kindly to yourself, you are learning something important about who you are.

These lessons do not stay only on the court. What you learn through basketball helps you in school, friendships, and everyday life. Learning to be patient, resilient, and confident is part of the player and person you are becoming.

Take a moment to reflect on your basketball journey so far. Answer honestly and take your time.

One thing basketball has taught me about my body:

____

____

____

One thing basketball has taught me about my mindset:

____

____

____

One thing basketball has taught me about my emotions:

____

____

____

One lesson from basketball I want to remember off the court

____

____

____

The lessons you learn in basketball can help
you both on and off the court.

LETTER TO MY FUTURE SELF

Write a short note to your future basketball self. You can include encouragement, reminders, goals, or anything you want yourself to remember about your journey. Write honestly and from the heart.

Dear Future Me,

FINAL REFLECTION: LOOKING AHEAD

Take a moment to think about what comes next on your basketball journey. Look ahead with hope and confidence, knowing you will keep learning and growing.

One thing I am excited about for my basketball journey:

____

____

____

____

____

One reminder I want to keep with me:

____

____

____

____

____

Your journey is still unfolding. Keep showing up,
keep believing in yourself, and remember how far
you have already come.

BONUS SECTION

FUN PAGES

This section is all about having fun, being creative, and celebrating your love for basketball. There are no right or wrong answers here. Draw, doodle, write, and enjoy.

DESIGN YOUR OWN
TEAM MASCOT

Draw and design a mascot for your dream team. Your mascot can be an animal, character, or anything that represents teamwork, energy, and confidence.

MASCOT NAME

MY GAME-DAY-SNACK DREAM

Design your perfect game-day snack.

What's on my plate:

____

Why I love it:

____

BASKETBALL BINGO

Watch for the moments on your bingo card and mark them when they happen. Get five in a row across, down, or diagonally to get BINGO.

High five from a teammate	Encouraging a teammate	Listening to the coach	Smiling during the game	Staying calm under pressure
Trying again after a mistake	Good pass	Calling for the ball	Celebrating a teammate's score	Sharing the ball
Hustle play	Strong defense		Running back on defense	Learning from a mistake
Laughing on the bench	Staying positive	Staying focused	Good sportsman-ship	Playing with confidence
Taking a deep breath	Helping someone up	Giving full effort	Team cheer	Having fun on the court

Basketball Basics Crossword

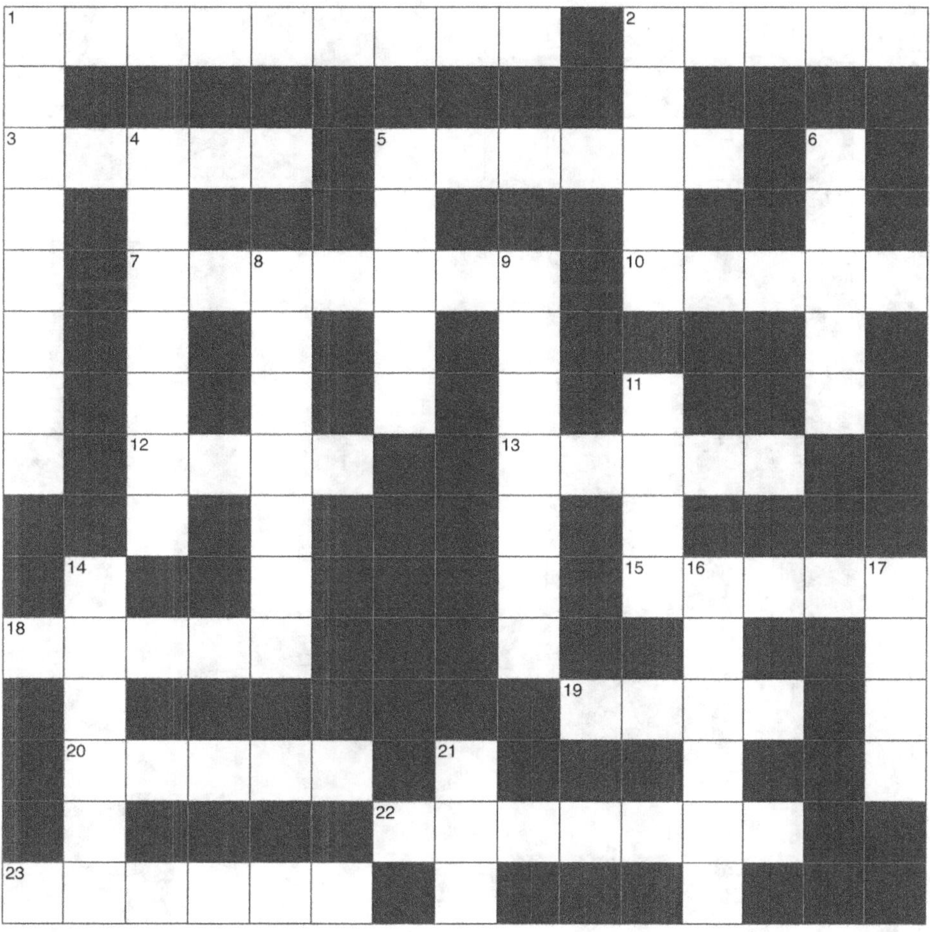

ACROSS

1 - The surface behind the basket
2 - A shot that goes in without touching the rim
3 - To get points by making a basket
5 - Usually the tallest player on the team
7 - A versatile player position on the court
10 - A close-range shot near the basket
12 - An attempt to make a basket
13 - Stopping an opponent's shot defensively
15 - Another name for the key area
18 - A common backcourt player position
19 - Throwing the ball to a teammate
20 - Keeping one foot planted while moving the other
22 - Trying to stop the other team from scoring
23 - Moving illegally without dribbling the ball

DOWN

1 - The end line of the basketball court
2 - Taking the ball from an opponent
4 - The team with possession of the ball
5 - The leader who guides the team
6 - The playing area for a basketball game
8 - Gaining possession of a missed shot
9 - Bouncing the ball to move it on the court
11 - The basket where players score points
14 - A shot taken while jumping in the air
16 - A pass leading directly to a score
17 - A group of players working together
21 - The rectangular area under the basket

Basketball Skills and Moves Crossword

ACROSS

1 - Jump shot while falling backward
4 - Pass the ball from out-of-bounds
8 - Intercept an opponent's pass or dribble
9 - Shot through the net without touching rim
15 - Challenge an opponent's shot
16 - Two defenders guard one offensive player
17 - Throw the ball to a teammate
18 - Change dribble direction quickly
20 - Aggressive defense across the court
21 - Turn on one foot while holding the ball
22 - Forcefully throw the ball through the hoop

DOWN

1 - High-arc shot over a defender
2 - Bounce the ball continuously
3 - Deceptive motion to trick a defender
5 - Position for a rebound
6 - Aggressively move toward the basket
7 - Prevent a shot from reaching the basket
8 - Attempt to score points at the basket
9 - Block a defender's path for a teammate
10 - Pause dribble to deceive a defender
11 - Quick step to fake a drive
12 - Gain possession after a missed shot
13 - Pass leading directly to a score
14 - Shot close to the basket, off the backboard
18 - Quick movement to get open
19 - Change direction while shielding the ball

Basketball Game Day Essentials Wordsearch

```
T O B R A S C O R E C N U O N N A O C P
O S A T F O E T T K E M I T F L A H C O
S S L U U R B R S E N C R R D E T H U P
U T L C O E U R I E F U B L H Y W N C C
T E D I L O R E L I I M D E H H L L T O
O K E O C E R B B D P O B T I S S C E R
K C K T E E B U B C I O S S E H H O P N
C I E H B I Z N S F A S T M O A C O A N
O T C O R Z E K G S O L H O S H M E O R
L P U D E B N M N H E E P E C L I R R T
C N O R S I D E L S E L S N R N T E N L
D C U E R C H R O S N A E N R Z K D A B
F Z T D E T C M A P M B O F E E S C F C
N J C R D E A Y C O S A R N N A K H C C
N U E D E R O N R K B S R E L N K U F Z
O O E R A C C Z L I A E E G F U Z E E H
E L O S S A P E H R E T R A O E O E R K
E E R A E E F P O M A S C O T R R F E S
B R E D N H Y E B S N A F S C B P E T R
J I R T C T I M E O U T H U P S E A E O
```

ANNOUNCER	DUNK	PROGRAM
BALL	FANS	REBOUND
BENCH	FOUL	REFEREE
BUZZER	HALFTIME	SCOREBOARD
CHEER	HOOP	SHOOT
CLOCK	JERSEY	SNEAKERS
COACH	MASCOT	TEAM
COURT	NET	TICKETS
DRIBBLE	PASS	TIMEOUT
DRINKS	POPCORN	WHISTLE

Basketball Stars and Positions Wordsearch

```
T P C I S N I E E E L E R I O M N S E A
O P U O L D I B L T I H F F A S R S N R
T M O C P I S E U O E H O S T D N I S B
F U O N N T A T W N C R S D N E D W M T
E J R D E D I L I N W I R C F U I L S L
E A R A E M G T E A S I R F N S N E B S
H C L R S W U B R T B E O K H N L R L E
N E T A D B A D C B K A A T P H O C O S
I K W D R N R S L F S E B C I O A O C F
T H A C E C D E V O A F I F N P O O K B
F P R L E F R R O D R N W K T K R H A S
P R A E E N E C N S E O W A O E O L L N
F N P S D O T N H I T C I O U O L I A R
P S O T S N N E S P O N D T C T R M N C
P R H I W R U C R E O F R E E N C N E R
G P A R P S N O D A H O N A T R U O C I
O M S T O M O A B B S J M P E C F L O C
C V N R E D A C E E E R I W I N N E R K
A P D N O T K H K E R L W M J C N E N L
E I D R R T A N C I M H N E E R M W N A
```

ASSIST	DRIBBLER	OFFENSE
BALL	DUNK	PASS
BENCH	FAN	REBOUNDER
BLOCK	FORWARD	ROOKIE
CAPTAIN	GUARD	SCORE
CENTER	HOOP	SHOOTER
CHAMPION	JUMP	STEAL
COACH	LEADER	SWISH
COURT	MVP	TEAM
DEFENSE	NET	WINNER

CROSSWORD AND WORDSEARCH ANSWERS

BASKETBALL BASICS CROSSWORD

BASKETBALL SKILLS AND MOVES CROSSWORD

BASKETBALL GAME DAY ESSENTIALS WORDSEARCH

BASKETBALL STARS AND POSITIONS WORDSEARCH

SHARE YOUR EXPERIENCE

Basketball is a journey you carry with you, on the court and beyond it. Every time you showed up, tried again, or chose to believe in yourself, you were building something meaningful. Those moments matter more than any score or stat.

There will be games you remember forever and others you will forget, but the confidence, courage, and resilience you are growing will stay with you. Keep trusting your effort, listening to your heart, and playing with joy.

If this workbook helped you feel supported, encouraged, or more confident in yourself, I would be grateful if you shared your experience.

📱 Scan the QR code below to leave a quick review on Amazon.
Your words could remind another player that she is not alone and that her journey is worth believing in.